Leaving A Legacy

Start Planting Seeds Today To Establish Your Own Legacy

❖

Brandie Forbes

DISCLAIMER

This information is provided and sold with the knowledge that the publisher and author do not offer any legal or other professional advice. In the case of a need for any such expertise consult with the appropriate professional. This book does not contain all information available on the subject. This book has not been created to be specific to any individual's or organizations' situation or needs. Every effort has been made to make this book as accurate as possible. However, there may be typographical and or content errors. Therefore, this book should serve only as a general guide and not as the ultimate source of subject information. This book contains information that might be dated and is intended only to educate and entertain. The author and publisher shall have no liability or responsibility to any person or entity regarding any loss or damage incurred, or alleged to have incurred, directly or indirectly, by the information contained in this book.

Thank you for downloading this book. Please review on Amazon for us so that I can make future versions even better. A portion of the proceeds from this book goes to American Cancer Society®. Thank you for you support. God bless.

Just for Downloading this book and showing your support, I wanna give you 2 of our other books, absolutely **FREE**. Just go to the link and subscribe and get **2 Free Books** for your support. Don't forget to give us **5 star Rating** so we can make better versions to help more people. Thank you guys for your support.

Click Here to Download-Free Website Traffic & How To Invest in The Stock Market

Table of Contents

Foreword 7

1. The Basics 9

2. Getting A Grip On Life 15

3. Be A Star 21

4. Things To Help 25

5. Get The Word Out 31

Wrapping Up 35

Foreword

Leaving a legacies isn't automatic; it is something that is carefully constructed.

You have to treasure the correct goals and ideals. This content tells you how you ought to go about it.

Chapter 1:

The Basics

Synopsis

Imparting a legacy is something most individuals do not consciously think about, and those that do, are thinking about a bigger picture, something that"s greater than life itself. However, how do you leave a legacy for other people to follow and peruse?

What You Should Know

Does the thought about leaving behind a legacy make you feel really low? Oh no, this isn't for me, I am not President Lincoln or Einstein or Mother Teresa!

Think once more. For a change, don"t think of such awesome internationally acclaimed icons of accomplishment. Think of somebody around you - your acquaintance or relation or co-worker at the office or your priest, simply anybody who is or was a part of your day-to-day life.

What do you instantaneously remember about him or her? Did he do something great for you or other people? Did she produce something special that did good things for other people? Did they battle some little injustice in the system and alter the rules for better?

So you recall that stern old James, your managing director at the factory was also a thoughtful and fair boss who was loved and respected by all your fellow workers.

It strikes you that it was your uncle John who led the fight to save the old movie house on your street from the wrecking ball and got it recorded as a heritage property. And your mother"s unbelievable apple pies are spoken of by each family for 4 blocks down the road, all because she liberally shared her recipe and egged on the young homemakers until they perfected the artistic creation of the apple pie!

There you are…that's a legacy! When people imprint their deeds in the hearts and minds of individuals around them, they leave behind a legacy. Now consider…what do individuals remember when they think of you right now? Great stuff? Foul stuff? Sorry stuff? Oh, you never gave it a thought, did you? Perhaps people around you don"t remember you the least bit.

Uh oh, that likely makes you feel even lower than before. However you now know what it means to leave a legacy, and how even the most modest individual may leave behind a legacy. So get started, bang into the game and begin doing your thing - those simple but astonishing deeds that will leave behind your legacy.

Starting small is the right way to start.

You've just celebrated your 60th birthday and you're feeling as rotten as hell. How come? Because you all of a sudden realize that you're not going to leave anything valuable or real behind.

Yes, you know you've been a great son, husband and dad, however what about those great legendary stories that are told about particular individuals? Will anybody talk about you in

Leaving A Legacy

proud awe of something awesome that you accomplished? Are you leaving behind a legacy?

I"m already an old granddad, you think, and what may I do today? Isn"t it too late? Come again, you said you are a granddad, did you? That itself is a most potent asset.

Have you observed that a lot of acquaintances around you always talk about their grandparents? Not that their grandma or grandpa built the Statue of Liberty or something, but merely simple matters. They talk about when grandpa took them fishing down at the river and the awesome time they had. Or the fact that in the sorry old days, granny took the pains to collect scraps of cloth from the local seamstress and stitched new pants for them shavers!

Are you spending any such quality time with your grandchildren? Are you going on adventures with them, or presenting them great advice? Something that they'll talk about in muted tones when recalling their childhood? A daughter pays tribute to the grandpa of her sons in the verse form below:-

"He loved everybody that's here, and a few he never met, a man of forbearance and forgivingness, I know we won't forget. My boys loved him dear, with simply a bushel and a peck, and never could they leave without a hug about the neck."

You have an immense repertoire of your life experiences that you are able to share with your grandchildren. You are able to bestow your work skills and your life skills to them, a little each day.

They'll learn from your errors and be inspired by your success and someday they'll say - "You know, my grandpa used to say…" That"s when you will know deep in your spirit, that you've become a "famous grandpa" and have left behind an awesome legacy.

Chapter 2:

Getting A Grip On Life

Synopsis

Individuals who leave rich legacies behind are mindful of the importance of the richest asset of all - time. One of the excellent motivational speakers of this century Rev Billy Graham states - "The legacy we leave isn't just in our possessions, but in the quality of our life story. ...The biggest waste in all of our world, which can't be recycled or reclaimed, is our waste of the time that God has given us every day."

Understand This

In the words of an anonymous sage -

"This is the start of a fresh day.

You have been given this day to utilize as you will. You are able to waste it or utilize it for good.

What you do now is crucial

Because you're exchanging a day of your life story for it. When tomorrow arrives, this day will be gone evermore; In its place is something that you've left behind...

Let it be something great."

You have always been worried about getting value for your cash when you go shopping. But are you acquiring value for the time in your life? Are the hours being wasted away in front of the idiot box? Are days passing pointlessly? Can you recall what you did 4 days ago?

If you can't, then you are casting aside the most cherished resource of your life story. Time is the most crucial building block of your legacy. Someday you might have a lot of cash and individuals working for you, but you'll have run out of time. You can"t borrow time. No one will loan it to you.

So the minute to begin working at your legacy is today.

Escape that couch and do one little thing that will stand for you - compose a page of prose, reach out to a destitute neighbor, send off a letter to your local newspaper about an issue that troubles you, teach the local youngsters how to play the sax, organize a community tidy up, invent a better drinking straw, shoot a video recording and upload it on YouTube...

You're the boss. You wear the trousers. For each day of your life, demand that you get your fair share of life and its payoffs. Give notice that henceforward you have taken control of your time!

You have to understand why you exist. There's some reason for you being here.

You have everything you need-a nice household, great food, a loving family, an awesome job atmosphere and great acquaintances. But still a pecking emptiness haunts your life. Clouds of anxiety still trouble your perfect life. What on earth may be missing from your life story?

Stephen R. Covey, among the most successful New Age gurus fills out the picture in this awesome saying -

Leaving A Legacy

There are particular things that are central to human fulfillment. The essence of these needs is seized in the phrase "to live, to love, to learn, to leave a legacy". The need to live is our tangible need for such things as food, apparel, shelter, economical-well being, and wellness.

The need to love is our social need to relate to others, to belong, to love and to be loved. The need to learn is our mental need to grow and to mature. And the need to leave a legacy is our spiritual need to have a sense of meaning, reason, personal congruence and contribution in our life.

You might observe that the first three needs of Live, Love and Learn are characteristics we share to some extent with all animal life on earth. But the 4th quality is unambiguously human. Only Man wishes to do something awesome in his lifetime, something that he or she may leave as a legacy. Only Man seeks a "sense of meaning" in his life. Only Man asks - how come I am here? How will I be remembered when I'm gone?

Among the most capital benefits you will gain from working consciously and deliberately on your legacy is a sense of meaning and reason in your life. This bright uplifting feeling will quickly wipe out any depressing thoughts of low self esteem.

You'll be buoyed by your own deeds and thoughts as you work steadily towards a tangible accomplishment each day. Throw away your Prozac, the euphoria of living a Legacy is here!

Chapter 3:

Be A Star

Synopsis

It has been stated, if you wish to leave a legacy that lasts for a long time, you ought to write a bestseller book or compose a hit song or construct a great structure.

In the past, producing such a work took a long time. More time would pass by before a book or poem or song or film spread to the remainder of the world and received the critical acknowledgement you have been praying or trusting for.

Viral

However in today"s world, one doesn't have to wait for ages to sell a million copies or wait for peer acknowledgement. We are in the era of digital video, Net and YouTube! We have immense resources at our fingertips with Google, Bing and Wikipedia.

Gifted persons like Olav Per Kindgren and younger personalities like "Fred Figglehorn" and Natalie Tyler Tran of Community Channel have millions of individuals enjoying watching their music and videos.

In today"s world, if you have something useful and entertaining to provide to the world, a video of your expression may spread virally across the world in days or even hours !

Simply imagine you shoot a video recording on your cell phone, edit it with some net software and upload it on YouTube. It spreads through acquaintances and friends of acquaintances and before you know it, you have produced a lasting legacy in the realms of cyberspace.

Virtual space it might be, but there are real individuals watching these video recordings and gaining and being inspired by them, so such a legacy is likewise very real and life-impacting.

However how may I compete on YouTube with those millions of people uploading day-to-day? The secret to this unique video that will go viral is YOU once again! You are different from all the billions of individuals on this planet and YOU have something different to say or do. Simply think well about what you are great at and begin planning a great video today. Get a camera and shoot yourself doing your special thing. And upload. And take it easy and watch your own little legacy go viral!

Chapter 4:

Things To Help

Synopsis

Begin now to be there tomorrow.

Leaving behind a legacy by the feats you do in your lifetime is really crucial. However how you share and transmit your worldly assets after you've passed on may likewise contribute tremendously to your legacy.

Get Started

Here are some steps you are able to take to accomplish a tangible and lasting legacy through your assets:-

Reflect wisely on your priorities and ready a will.

Leave behind a gift or a particular fund for your favorite not-for-profit organization. See to it that you likewise name alternate beneficiaries, should those organizations cease to exist.

If you've pension plans or life insurance policies in surplus of loved ones' needs, bequeath part of that amount to a charity that you're acquainted with. Each asset- be it cash, real property, personal belongings and memorabilia ought to be accounted for in your will.

Arrange scholarships for needy pupils or other people in niches that might be neglected by State funds.

Decide whether you want anonymity or that these pledges ought to be in your name or the names of your parent or youngster or any other individual or institution. Encourage acquaintances and family members to contribute to such scholarships and charity funds. Donate your most personal asset - your body - to the State, to enable organ transplantations after your death.

What would you do to establish your legacy?

The Egyptians left behind the Great Pyramids as their legacy. Gustave Eiffel is recollected for the Eiffel Tower. Elvis Presley and the Beatles presented us hundreds of hit songs while Bob Dylan continues to add to his already colossal legacy! What is your legacy going to be?

Here are some ideas to get you working on your legacy straight off at this very second:-

Compose your book.

Don"t worry about it having to contend with Stephen Covey or Stephen King or any other Stephen! Simply let it be about your own experiences and your point of view. It may be a novel or a non-fiction book about your area of expertise.

Even if you're no authority, go to the library or browse the Net and come up with ideas and info to fill a whole book. Simply give all that text your own twist.

Construct your own home.

You were going to construct your new home anyway right? Let it be something unique in your neighborhood or even in the state or country or the world! Why settle for a commonplace architectural design?

Utilize your own ideas; utilize radically different "green" materials! Let it stick out as your legacy to architecture by reflecting your thoughts. Simply think outside the masonry box!

Teach your youngsters well.

As the song by Crosby Stills & Nash goes: "Teach your youngsters well…And feed them on your dreams…The one they picked, the one you'll know by."

Invite the shavers in your neighborhood and teach them a fresh skill or coach them at baseball, free of charge. They'll never forget you and who knows, you might just be mentoring the next Babe Ruth or Willie Mays!

Invent something.

It may be something as simple as a better paper clip or as big as a better Hadron Collider. Apply your brain to an issue and allow your subconscious mind to pop up a solution. Make sure to apply for a patent, even if it's an easy little invention. Remember Post-Its!

Travel the land with a message.

Take a significant issue, little or big, and take some cash and get on the trail. Explain the issue to individuals and lobby for reform. The media will catch up on you and you'll be heard. And you'll meet tons of new individuals and see loads of new places. That little bit of reform will be your legacy.

Chapter 5:

Get The Word Out

Synopsis

You have to let individuals know what you are doing.

Make It Known

Serge Roetheli of Switzerland started his run around the world in 2000 at the age of forty-seven, eventually covering thirty-seven countries in six continents.

Rosie Swale-Pope of England started running at fifty-seven years of age and got across over 20,000 miles in her run around the globe.

Paul Staso, an ultra endurance athlete and founder of PACE Fitness Foundation who has likewise run across the United

States, states that over 200 individuals have run across the U.S.A., with a dozen or so in reality running solo. What guts!

What is it that makes individuals run across nations and even the world? In the renowned film "Forrest Gump", the main character played by Tom Hanks gets up one morning and begins running, traversing the U.S.A. 3/4 over 5 years.

When asked why he ran, Gump says - "Because I felt like running". There's something inside us that frequently makes us want to leave our mediocre lives behind and simply run free. And in that free run of our life, we may produce a new legacy.

Brian Stark, an English teacher who ran across the country, has this to say - "I thought my body would be a shrinking mass after a thousand miles, but it kept becoming stronger."

A lot of individuals have coupled their running or travelling across nations or countries with a distinguishable message that they wish to spread wherever they go. So you are able to Run for Peace or "run to raise funds for cancer research" or "run for reform".

If physical limits do not permit you to run, you are able to drive or simply travel all over, holding meetings or talking to individuals to spread your unique message. It is not uncommon to hear of people packing some stuff onto a bicycle in India and travelling all over with a simple notice on the bike"s front. It's a simple and humble act, but it touches the hearts of individuals and it brings about change. That simple man on a cycle is producing his own legacy.

Wrapping Up

18th century America tells us of a man called Johnny Appleseed who went all over the earth planting apple seeds. After he had traveled to the finish of his journey, he would return along the same path, minding the little trees that had grown and plating fresh ones.

An immense network of nurseries and grown trees stands nowadays as the legacy of John Chapman, an American pioneer gardener, who came to be called the legendary John Appleseed.

Johnny Appleseed left behind an estate of over 1,200 acres of useful nurseries, worth millions even then, and far more now. Johnny Appleseed Elementary School today stands in Leominster, Massachusetts, his birthplace.

Leaving A Legacy

You are able to begin planting seeds today to establish your own legacy. You are able to take this lesson literally and begin planting seeds and trees in your neighborhood or all over your state. The surroundings will be richer for your action and the communities around those trees will of course benefit from them.

If you plant an acorn now, you might not live to see it become a behemoth oak tree, but your descendants and those who take shelter in the shade of that tree will give thanks to you and your legacy.

Or you are able to take a metaphorical view and begin planting the seeds of education in the garden of young brains. Teach young individuals whatever you know best - a technical skill, moral lessons, share your life skills.

Then nurture them on a regular basis by following up and boosting your students to accomplish great ideals. Trim their wayward branches and fertilize their roots with continuing advice.

Each great achiever tells of a mentor, somebody who educated and inspired them in their lives and careers. You are able to be that sage in young people"s lives.

And in time you'll be known as Timothy Oaktree or Guitar Greg or Viola Vineyard or even Football Floyd! It doesn"t take a mastermind to leave a legacy behind, but it does ask a lot of additional things. By now, you have a more clear-cut picture of what leaving a legacy means. Have fun applying the techniques mentioned in the eBook.

Printed in Great Britain
by Amazon.co.uk, Ltd.,
Marston Gate.